# How to Make Money as an Ar

**By Chris Guthrie**

http://ChrisGuthrieBooks

## Disclaimer and Terms of Use

DISCLAIMER AND TERMS OF USE AGREEMENT

The author and publisher of this book and the accompanying materials have used their best efforts in preparing this book. The author and publisher make no representation or warranties with respect to the accuracy, applicability, fitness, or completeness of the contents of this book. The information contained in this book is strictly for informational purposes. Therefore, if you wish to apply ideas contained in this book, you are taking full responsibility for your actions.

Every effort has been made to accurately represent this book and it's potential. Even though this industry is one of the few where one can write their own check in terms of earnings, there is no guarantee that you will earn any money using the techniques and ideas in these materials. Examples in these materials are not to be interpreted as a promise or guarantee of earnings. Earning potential is entirely dependent on the person using our book, ideas and techniques. We do not purport this as a "get rich scheme." any claims made of actual earnings or examples of actual results can be verified upon request. Your level of success in attaining the results claimed in our materials depends on the time you devote to the knowledge and various skills. Since these factors differ according to individuals, we cannot guarantee your success or income level. Nor are we responsible for any of your actions

Materials in our product and our website may contain information that includes or is based upon forward-looking statements within the meaning of the securities litigation reform act of 1995. Forward-looking statements give our expectations or forecasts of future events. You can identify these statements by the fact that they do not relate strictly to historical or current facts. They use words such as "anticipate," "estimate," "expect," "project," "intend," "plan," "believe," and other words and terms of similar meaning in connection with a description of potential earnings or financial performance.

**Table of Contents:**

# 1. Introduction and My Background Story

My name is Chris Guthrie and in this book **I'm going to teach you with real life examples how I've generated over $100,000 in commissions from Amazon's affiliate program** over the past few years, **sold one of my top Amazon websites in a deal worth six figures** and then leveraged these successes into growing my business into other areas as well. By the end of this book you should have a clear understanding of what elements are commonly found in websites successfully monetized using Amazon's affiliate program so that you can employ these elements in building your own successful websites.

I've been a full time internet entrepreneur since October 13, 2009. That was the day I lost my job. This was completely unexpected but when it happened I was already earning more money from my Amazon Associates account than I was at my day job. I decided that day to dive into my online business full time. I had spent several years prior trying out a wide variety of internet business models and failed miserably at nearly everything I tried. It wasn't until 2009 that I started earning respectable money online (i.e. over $1,000 per month) and every year since I lost my job my income has continued to grow and is comfortably inside the six figure range. Years after initially getting started with Amazon's affiliate program I now earn money from a variety of different places but I intend to help you clearly understand what key elements are found in a website monetized by Amazon's affiliate program.

I use Wordpress (a free content management system) to power all of my websites and as a thank you for buying this book I'm giving free access to my Amazon Wordpress plugin that allows you to more quickly and easily create affiliate links without going to Amazon.com to create them. It cost me several thousand dollars to develop and is a huge time saver. You can get free access to that software here for use on all of your Wordpress powered websites:

http://chrisguthriebooks.com/free-software/

Now before we get further into the strategies I've used to earn money from Amazon I'd like to explain why I chose to make money using

Amazon's affiliate program as opposed to some of the other ways to make money online.

# 2. Why I Chose to Become an Amazon Affiliate

As a member of Amazon's affiliate program **you have the ability to recommend millions of products available for sale on Amazon.com** ranging from books to video games and everything in between and to receive a commission if someone purchases a product after clicking through your affiliate link. I'll discuss the various strategies to make money with Amazon's affiliate program later in this book, but **the vast product catalog allows you to choose from tens of thousands of niches to work in**.

Before using Amazon's affiliate program I made money by building popular websites that got tons of traffic and then I leveraged that traffic into income from ad clicks (i.e. Google Adsense). Unfortunately, this only ever made me a small income and certainly would not have allowed me to leave my day job.

An example of one of my ultimately flawed websites is **GamingVidz.com** – this was my first moderately successful website that at the height of its popularity (mid 2000's) managed to generate **only $500 per month** with Google Adsense despite garnering over **500,000 page views per month** (which is a relatively large amount of traffic). It was only after building GamingVidz.com and trying to make money from ads by sheer amounts of traffic that I realized there had to be a better way to make money. Sure there are websites around that make money from ads simply by focusing on getting a lot of traffic, but I recognized that another method could be to build websites that targeted niches where people were already looking to buy products. That way I could recommend products on my website that people were already looking to buy and earn a nice commission off each sale rather than hoping that the people that came to my website would click an ad on the sidebar so I could get 5 cents from Adsense. Don't get me wrong, I still make money from Adsense through various websites, but what appealed to me about Amazon was the chance at larger rewards for sales that I could refer.

I could go on sharing why recommending products on Amazon.com through their affiliate program is an effective monetization strategy but I'm sure you get my point by now so let's move onto the next section.

# 3. What Makes a Successful Amazon Income Generating Website?

Alright, so I've already covered my background and explained why I chose to participate in Amazon's affiliate program but if you're a complete beginner I'd like to lay it all out so that you understand everything before we get into specific strategies for building websites.

### 3a. How I make money

I make money by building niche and authority style websites that target one or more keyword phrases that people search for in Google – the more someone searches for a phrase the better (but also the more competition there generally is). When people come to these websites they can read articles that I've written articles with affiliate links embedded within the content. When someone clicks those links they are taken to Amazon.com. After someone clicks one of my affiliate links as long as they buy an item in the next 24 hours I receive a commission for their purchase. I like to buy domain names that encompass the keyword phrase I'm targeting (or at least a portion of it). For example, one niche Amazon website I have is http://wirelesshdmi.net and I build that site to target the keyword phrase "wireless hdmi" which receives thousands of searches per month in Google's search engine. **That website has generated nearly $5,000 in commissions since I created it a few years ago.**

| Tracking ID ▼ | Clicks ▽ | Items Ordered ▽ | Items Shipped ▽ | Shipped Items Revenue ▽ | Advertising Fees ▽ |
|---|---|---|---|---|---|
| wirelesshdmi-20 | 48349 | 1413 | 1338 | $106,982.09 | **$4,760.39** |

The goal behind each website is to build something that ranks in Google and other various search engines for the primary and secondary keywords that I'm targeting. In late September of 2012 Google updated their algorithm to reduce the bonus that EMD or exact match domains provided in regards to SEO. So the example "wireless hdmi" website that I've shown you using an exact match keyword domain name doesn't mean you need to go out and do the same thing. In fact, there is little reason to go out and spend a lot to buy a nice exact match keyword domain name if they aren't available to register because Google is treating all domains on the same playing field now. This just illustrates Google's continually changing algorithm and their desire to only allow the best sites to rise to the top search engine results.

*Important Note: Google uses hundreds if not thousands of factors to influence search engine rankings and the way in which they rank websites continually changes. In the next section I'll discuss the strategy for more sites with lower quality or less sites that are higher quality.*

### 3b. Google ranking basics – link building

One of the primary key factors that can influence rankings in Google is the number of links that point towards that website. **Crudely explained, links are basically counted as votes with the more votes a website has the more valuable it will appear in Google's eyes and the better search engine rankings it likely will have.** Now things are much more complex than this because each link isn't created equal in the eyes of Google. Paying $5 for someone to create 100 forum links pointed at your website fromhttp://fiverr.com is not nearly as valuable as getting your website mentioned on http://engadget.com because you found out when a hot new product was recently listed on Amazon.com and you were the first tech site to report on it. I've used both of these tactics in the past with the latter being more effective, but obviously more time consuming.

In this book I intentionally want to steer clear of sharing any definitive strategies for link building precisely because of how fast Google updates their algorithm. Any strategy I share in this book could be effective for the next 24 hours or maybe the next 12 months from the time you've read it. In fact, less than 48 hours after I published this book I had to go back in and make some changes because of a Google algorithm update. With that said, there are some very simple guidelines you can follow if you want to limit your risk of Google deranking your websites:

**The less effort you've expended to acquire a link the more likely it is to have less value over time in the eyes of Google**

Going back to my earlier example clearly paying $5 for a pack of 100 forum links is less valuable than getting a link from one of the top tech blogs in the world because the forum links only cost me $5 and the link from http://engadget.com required me to closely follow a market and watch when highly anticipated products popped up for sale on Amazon.com and then send an email to their tips section in hopes that they'd pick it up.

Link building strategies also vary based on the type of website you want to build so the next thing I'd like to cover are the differences between niche and authority style websites as well as the pros and cons of each.

# 4. Should I Build a Niche or Authority Website?

I've made tens of thousands of dollars from Amazon's affiliate program from both a combination of niche (aka smaller + generally lower quality) and authority style websites (aka larger + higher quality). Before we get into the fundamental aspects of website creation (picking a niche, writing content, etc.), I would like to discuss niche and authority style websites and address the pros and cons of each style so that you can decide what you might be interested in building for yourself.

### 4a. The Pros Of Niche Websites

Niche websites are typically 5 – 20 page websites that focus on a much smaller target keyword that might receive only a thousand or so searches per month. The actual content and construction of these websites can generally be completed through outsourced article websites such as http://textbroker.com, http://elance.com andhttp://odesk.com. This means that the work you have to invest in the site in order to create and maintain it can be fairly low. Remember the http://wirelesshdmi.net website I mentioned before? I wrote only 5 articles for that site when I created it and built just a few dozen links. Since then, like I mentioned previously, **it has made me nearly $5,000 in commissions**.

### 4b. The Cons of Niche Websites

One of the biggest trends I've seen in 2012 that will continue into 2013 and beyond is the speed with which Google is updating their algorithm with major fundamental shifts in search engine optimization (SEO). The algorithm that Google uses determines which websites rank for various keywords. You can view a chart outlining all of the various updates from SEOmoz here: http://www.seomoz.org/google-algorithm-change

The problem with niche websites is that ultimately you have to be playing the numbers game by building a lot of websites (most will fail, some will do alright and even less will do great). Additionally with niche websites you must stay on top of changes in Google's algorithm and because they're performing so many updates it takes a lot of effort to be constantly testing and tracking various link building methods across your network of niche websites.

I don't think that niche websites are dead or dying, but the question you need to ask yourself is if you want to spend your time battling all of the changes with Google or just spend more time and effort building a higher quality authority style website. It's clear that Google is constantly taking steps to improve the websites found in the top search results and I believe that higher quality niche sites will be crucial for success moving forward.

### 4c. The Pros of Authority Websites

One of the best benefits of building larger authority style websites is the greater income potential and stability in traffic levels and earnings. One of the larger websites that I built and later sold was a product review website that you can read about in this free blog post I wrote:

**"How I Sold A Website For Six Figures"**

http://entrepreneurboost.com/how-to-sell-a-website/

With this website I was able to collect a nice monthly income and then sell the website for a lump sum as well. With authority websites they are generally easier to sell for higher income multiples because of their quality level.

The other benefit as you grow an authority website is that if you spend 2 hours a day working on the website (for example) and get to 100,000 page views per month it is entirely possible to continue spending only 2 hours per day working on the website and to grow that page view count to 200,000 per month. Over time you'll have written more articles, ranked for more keywords in Google, your email list grows larger and more people start sharing your content through social media sources. **The point I'm trying to illustrate is that you can literally be spending the same amount of time on the website in January and twelve months later be making twice as much.**

With niche websites, generally speaking, once you hit the #1 search result for your target keyword that's the best you're going to ever do with that website.

### 4d. The Cons of Authority Websites

The flip side of building larger authority style websites is that your eggs are all in one basket so to speak. All your work will be consolidated into a few websites (or maybe even just one). So, if you get comfortable with a certain level of monthly income and something happens to affect your traffic or income the hit will hurt a lot more.

The other obvious downside is that authority websites take a lot of work. I flew down to the consumer electronics expo just to cover the event live on my authority style website to try and bring even more credibility to the quality of my website. There's no way around it – authority websites simply take more time and effort to successfully build.

Ultimately, you have to decide which website style or combination of styles will work best for you. I hope that this analysis between both niche and authority style websites will help you to determine what you're most interested in going after. Having said all of that, I'd like to switch gears and discuss another crucial element to your success with Amazon affiliate websites: **how to find a niche market**.

# 5. How to Find a Niche Market:

**This is the most important step and the place where most people fail.** Finding a niche is a task that can be solved in a couple different ways. There are valuable free and premium tools that you can use to conduct your research. When I first got started in this business I only used free tools (partly because I didn't know any better) so I'd like to cover those first and I want to be clear that you don't have to pay for anything other than web hosting and domain names to do what I'm teaching.

## 5a. The number one free tool you need for niche research

The Google Adwords Keyword Planner is the best free tool for niche research. It's what I used when I first started and I still use it today from time to time when I just need a quick check on some keyword data. You can access the tool by going to: http://adwords.google.com/ko/KeywordPlanner or just search "Google Adwords Keyword Planner" you'll need to create a free Google Adwords account to use the tool, but after that there are just a few steps to take.

### Step 1: Enter your keyword (or keywords) into the search box.

Your product or service

| wireless hdmi | Get ideas |

| Ad group ideas | Keyword ideas | | ⬇ Download | Add all (801) |

| Search terms | Avg. monthly searches ? | Competition ? | Avg. CPC ? | Ad impr. share ? | ✎ ▾ |
|---|---|---|---|---|---|
| wireless hdmi | 40,500 | High | $0.62 | 0% | |

1 - 1 of 1 keywords ▾   ‹   ›

We'll continue with the example I used earlier, the keyword phrase "wireless hdmi." For that phrase, I'd simply enter in my target keyword phrase.  Or, if you don't have an idea for a keyword or phrase yet, simply enter in various keywords in areas that you're interested in.

**Step 2: Next we need to look at the avg monthly searches provided by the tool**

As you can see from the earlier image, there are 40,500 searches per month for the keyword "wireless hdmi." The competition for this keyword phrase is now "High" but when I first built this site the competition was "Low." Another element to consider is the approximate CPC (cost per click). CPC basically tells you how profitable the potential niche is. I generally don't pay a lot of attention to this number. Instead, I look at the types of products that I can sell from Amazon.com on my potential website. In the case of "wireless hdmi" the typical product sells for around $100 - $200 which will give me a decent commission of between $4 and $18 depending on what commission rate I'm at for the month (more on that to come later in this guide).

**Step 3: Didn't find a good keyword?**

The nice part about the Google Adwords Keyword Planner is that while you may not get the results you're looking for in the initial words you put into the search Google will still provide you with hundreds of related keyword ideas and their total search volume.

| Keyword (by relevance) | Avg. monthly searches ? | Competition ? | Avg. CPC ? | Ad impr. share ? | |
| --- | --- | --- | --- | --- | --- |
| wireless hdmi transmitter | 4,400 | High | $0.81 | 0% | » |
| wireless hdmi cable | 1,600 | High | $0.36 | 0% | » |
| wireless hdmi extender | 480 | High | $0.71 | 0% | » |
| wireless hdmi adapter | 880 | High | $0.75 | 0% | » |
| gefen wireless hdmi | 210 | High | $2.82 | 0% | » |
| iogear wireless hdmi | 590 | High | $0.48 | 0% | » |

So you might find a keyword like "wireless hdmi transmitter" has a decent search volume of 4,400 searches per month (I like to see at the very least 1,000 searches per month) and you could build a small niche website around that term instead.

Legal Disclaimer: You might have noticed in the previous picture that company name keywords such as "gefen wireless hdmi" and "iogear wireless hdmi" popped up.**DO NOT** buy domain names using copyrighted product and company names. You can get into legal trouble.

It is acceptable, however, to write an article like "Best Belkin Wireless HDMI Transmitters" on your website about wireless hdmi products.

### 5b. What types of keywords should you target?

Product oriented keywords do well, but one strategy that I've used to great effect is product review oriented keywords. The people that search for a term like "baseball bat reviews" are likely close to making a buying decision so their traffic is more valuable. That's why I'm a big fan of product review oriented websites. Here's an example of a product review website that I own: http://3dtvreviews.org.  This site has **generated me nearly $7,000 in income from Amazon.**

| Tracking ID ▼ | Clicks ▽ | Items Ordered ▽ | Items Shipped ▽ | Shipped Items Revenue ▽ | Advertising Fees ▽ |
|---|---|---|---|---|---|
| 3dtv01-20 | 16593 | 427 | 403 | $104,736.98 | **$4,400.77** |
| 3dtvcompare-20 | 12010 | 264 | 256 | $57,936.27 | **$2,474.94** |

This is the type of website that I could potentially grow into a bigger earning website, but lately I've been trying to focus on larger websites in an effort to get better value for my time. Because of this, I could see selling 3dtvreviews.org.  **I originally bought the website from someone for only $500!** Buying websites as a method for increasing Amazon income is another strategy I've employed on numerous occasions and I've even written a book all about buying websites which you can check out here:http://chrisguthriebooks.com/book2

### 5c. Alternative premium keyword research tool

Premium keyword research tools are designed to help you save time during the research process; however, I don't want to spend a lot of time discussing how to use these tools because I don't want you to think that you have to buy them, especially if you are just starting out. With that said, here is my top recommendation:

**Long Tail Pro** – I've know Spencer - the creator behind this tool - and we've even partnered on a few projects in the past so I was able to get a discount for you:

http://chrisguthriebooks.com/longtailprodiscount ($30 off discount link)

I got my start using the free Google Adwords Keyword Tool (which was retired in fall 2013 and replaced with the Google Adwords Keyword Planner). Long Tail Pro is how I do most of my research now because the tool helps to automate a lot of the keyword research steps including generating multiple keywords at once, finding domain names, check rank of websites, and a whole lot more. The point is that if you're serious about building websites and want to save time during the research process Long Tail Pro can help – but you can just use the free tools instead.

### 5d. Domain name you want not available?

One of the common things I hear from beginners is that the domains they look for are always taken. Well, for starters, I recommend either the .com, the .net or the .org when building niche websites. If you're trying to build an authority style website I recommend the .com and if necessary to choose a branded style domain name. What does "engadget" mean anyway? They just made up a word and then focused on building one of the best tech blogs in the world.  Now, if you're sticking with niche websites and your first choice .com, .net and .org are taken, another strategy that you can use is to add keyword modifiers such as "best baseball bats" instead of just "baseball bats" or "buy baseball bats." Ultimately you just want to make sure that the domain you choose to buy sounds right if spoken aloud. So to use a bad example you wouldn't want to use a keyword or buy a domain name like "baseball bats buy"

I use http://GoDaddy.com, http://Moniker.com and a few others for domain name purchases (they're basically all selling the same thing). If you buy through GoDaddy just do a quick search for "GoDaddy Promo Codes" and use those before you buy your domains – that and don't buy any of the upsells they offer except for perhaps domain privacy.

### 5e. Determining the competition for your target keyword phrase

I touched on this briefly when mentioning Long Tail Pro, but you can quickly and easily determine keyword competition by using their software. However, if you want to do it manually for free, here is how.

**Step 1: Google the keyword phrase you're looking to rank for**

**Step 2: Look at the websites on page 1 of your target keyword phrase**

**Step 3: Ask yourself "Can I build a better website than those that are currently ranking?"**

This may sound like a silly or overly simple way to do this, but you have to understand that Google exists to enhance a user's experience and more now than ever if you're not going to try and build a better website (in every sense of the word – i.e. better content, higher quality links etc.) than the existing websites currently ranking it's likely a niche that isn't worth targeting. I'd use a real life search results page example, but because they're always fluctuating depending on when you read this book you might not understand the example so I'll have to use a hypothetical example:

So, if you for example search for "Wireless HDMI" and you see a handful of Google YouTube videos, a few random blog posts and some online retailers ranking for the keyword I've found that those types of websites aren't as difficult to compete with. Where things get more difficult is when in the Google search results you do the same search for "Wireless HDMI" and every result you see is clearly targeting the "Wireless HDMI" keyword with their page titles. (Again if all this sounds a bit too involved or difficult, you can always consider the "harder road" and go after building an authority style website instead). Now that you understand some of the key elements in researching a niche or authority style website I'd like to take some time to discuss the actual creation process of building a niche or authority style website.

# 6. How to Create a Niche or Authority Website

Some of the technical aspects of this process may freeze some of you into inaction, but I don't want that to happen. The hosting provider I recommend has very helpful support staff and online wikis and I am confident you can do this! The company I use for hosting my own website portfolio and recommend to others is HostGator

Remember what I said earlier? When I started I didn't pay for any extra tools or software (although I didn't really know any better at the time) but the one thing I did have to pay for is web hosting because I needed to have access to a web server that would host my content. **You can't build a business on a free blog** – sure, there are a handful of large blogs hosted on BlogSpot out there, but many times these blogs are transitioned over to their own domain name and hosting eventually. The primary reason for using your own hosting is because you are in more control of your website and it would be more difficult to sell a free blog.

**6a. No pressure bonus offer – free Wordpress theme and bonus video training**

Look, I bet you've read a couple marketing related Kindle books before and I'm sure you've seen the authors are trying to sell you additional products (many times stuff you don't need). Now, I don't have any problem with recommending products that I personally use, but as I stated earlier, the one thing you absolutely must have is web hosting. So, if you sign up for web hosting using my coupon for HostGator, I'll get a commission for recommending you a service that you absolutely need and as a thank you from me I'll give you free access to my powerful Azon Wordpress Theme which is a theme that I use on http://wirelesshdmi.net, http://3dtvreviews.org and a bunch of other websites. I'll also give you access to some additional Amazon video training.

Step 1: Go to http://entrepreneurboost.com/hostgator and use the coupon code "**kindlechris**" (no quotes) when you place your order

Step 2: Send an email to support@nicheprofitcourse.com with the domain you used at sign up and I'll get you hooked up with the Wordpress theme and bonus training.

I have been a HostGator user for several years and I'm very pleased with them. Even if you don't take advantage of my offer they're a great hosting company to use for your niche or authority style websites. Now let's talk about the actual construction of your website.

### 6b. How to set up your website

Wordpress is the platform I use for every single website that I currently run. There are a plethora of continually updated videos being shared online that you can watch to see how to use Wordpress and the installation with most web hosting providers (HostGator included) is very simple. When you first purchase hosting your provider will email you with name server settings for your web hosting account. Take both of these name server URLs, log into your GoDaddy account, click the Domain Manager link and then click on the name servers button for domain name you just purchased (the process will be similar for other domain name providers). Simply input the two name server URL's from your email into the box below.

*Note: Your name servers will be different than mine. Also, if you buy the domain direct from HostGator you might be able to skip this step. Remember, support can help you with all of these steps.*

### 6c. How to install Wordpress

Go back to your HostGator email and click the link to go to your hosting control panel and log in. You'll be presented with a screen with various options. Scroll down to this section (near the bottom) and click "Fantastico De Luxe"

**Step 1:** From this screen click the Wordpress link on the left column.

**Step 2:** You'll be presented with an option to install Wordpress on a specific domain name. Click the install option and select the domain you wish to install Wordpress on along with the applicable settings.

**Step 3:** Be sure to write down your admin username and password as you'll need this to be able to log into your newly created Wordpress blog.

### 6d. Creating more Wordpress blogs

After you've created your first blog for the domain name you selected when you created your hosting account you'll need to do a few extra steps for each new blog you create.

So, log back into your HostGator Control Panel, scroll down to this section and click "**Addon Domains**" (if you're setting up the first blog in your hosting account you may be able to skip this step)

| Subdomains | Addon Domains | Parked Domains | Redirects | Simple DNS Zone Editor |
|---|---|---|---|---|

### Fill out the applicable details:

**Addon Domains**

*An addon domain allows you to reach a sub-domain when entering the name of the addon domain into a browser. This means that you can host additional domains from your account, if allowed by your hosting provider. Addon Domains Subdomains are relative to your account's home directory. The icon signifies your home directory which is*

*/home/guthrie.*

**Create an Add-on Domain**

New Domain Name: 

Subdomain/Ftp Username: 

Document Root: /

Password: 

Password (Again): 

Strength (why?): | Very Weak (0/100) | Password Generator

Add Domain

Hint: This feature must be enabled for your account before you can use it. Addon Domains will not be functional unless the domain name is registered with a valid registrar and configured to point to our DNS servers.

You're done! Now simply repeat the steps on the previous page (go to Fantastico De Luxe, Click Wordpress, Choose a domain to install Wordpress on etc.). If you're confused by any of these steps or just have questions about the bonus offer I've shared simply contact me here: http://entrepreneurboost.com/contact.

Alright, now that you've set up your first niche or authority style website you're going to need to create some content for it.

# 7. How to Write Content for your Blog

I like to write both review oriented articles and general information articles for the blogs that I create. To come up with general information article ideas I just pick keywords that surround the primary keyword I'm targeting.

### 7a. How to come up with content ideas

I simply go back to my initial keyword research search in Google Adwords Keyword Tool and scroll through the hundreds of extra results looking for other frequently searched phrases that relate to my niche. Remember these?

| Number of Products Shipped/Downloaded in a Given Month** | Volume–Based Advertising Fee Rates for General Products |
|---|---|
| 1–6 | 4.00% |
| 7–30 | 6.00% |
| 31–110 | 6.50% |
| 111–320 | 7.00% |
| 321–630 | 7.50% |
| 631–1570 | 8.00% |
| 1571–3130 | 8.25% |
| 3131+ | 8.50% |

Now, after pulling these results I have a list of 800 keyword ideas that I can use outright for article titles (e.g. "wireless hdmi transmitter" which is the keyword phrase I used to create this article: http://www.wirelesshdmi.net/wireless-hdmi-transmitter/ )

*Note: if you visit that URL – yes that content could be greatly improved but I didn't want to make any changes to the site to make it look better than it was before.*

Using these keyword ideas from Google to come up with possible articles you can write is very effective because you know that even if someone gets onto your website by some other means they very well could be interested in "wireless hdmi transmitters" since 4,400 people search for that term locally every month. This shortcut is just a quick way to avoid writer's block. Other great article formats include **"7 best 'insert your product niche' for under '$x' dollars"** because you're showing your visitor that you've done the work for them and found the best product for them within a price range.

### 7b. Write product review articles

As I've said before, product review style websites work very well for Amazon monetization because the people who are coming to these websites are already interested in buying a product in that niche. Even if your website isn't specifically a product review website like http://3dtvreviews.org you can still write reviews of the top products related to your niche.

### "But what if I can't actually review the product?"

That's a valid question and there a couple ways you can do this. For starters, if it is just a niche website and you can still write a review of the product by talking about its specifications and features. If for example you're trying to write a review on a 3D TV you could talk about the size of the TV, the resolution, the overall review star score on Amazon, the refresh rate, the advanced TV features such as picture in picture etc.

### 7c. How do you get demo products to review?

If you're building an authority style website and want to physically review the products (perhaps via video review) then you can contact companies to see if they can ship you a demo unit for your website. I routinely did this for the website I sold in a deal worth six figures.

For example: Let's say you want to review the latest Samsung device (I don't care what it is) simply Google "Samsung press contact" "Samsung press releases" etc. and search through the listings until you get someone's specific email address. I've found contacts by reading press releases finding out which person wrote it and then directly reaching out to them. If the press release just mentions their media website I'll go to that website, search around and if I'm not able to find an individual person I'll simply call their main phone line. The way I approach the conversation is very simple. I just say **"Hello, I'm Chris Guthrie and I run X website. I'd like to speak with someone that can provide me demo products to review on my website"** and this works very well. I've even used this strategy of reaching out to companies to get them to give me free products to give away to my readers – after all, they're getting relatively inexpensive exposure to my readers and I'm getting something free that I can give to my readers for some free value.

My point is that if you truly want to build an authority style website around one specific topic and build it up to something that people view as an important and trusted source of information, you can do that. You just need to hustle a bit when you're first starting out and the examples I've shared above are all things I did in the beginning.

### 7d. How to get content written for your website

When I first started out I wrote all of my own content, but since then I've tried to become less of a jack of all trades and more of a specialist at the few things I'm really good at. If you don't want to write your own content these are some of the places that I've used to have content written that have worked for me:

http://TextBroker.com – This is a website where you can request a certain quality level of writing, the topic you want, and anything else you can use to specify the type of article you want written. Most articles I've had written here fall between the 3 and 4 star level and were more than adequate for what I needed.

http://Odesk.com / http://Elance.com – These are marketplaces that you can use to hire people for a variety of tasks. I've used Odesk much more than Elance and more so for programming jobs, but you can also use these websites to find writers to hire.

http://jobs.problogger.net – This is a marketplace specifically for hiring bloggers. I've used this job board 3 or 4 times to hire bloggers for some of my higher quality authority style websites. It's a cheap fee to place a listing and I've gotten some great candidates from it.

But enough about writing content, I'd like to get to some real practical advice and discuss specific examples and strategies that you can use on your website to improve your chances at getting Amazon commissions and we'll do that in the next section.

# 8. How to Make Money with Amazon.com: Linking Strategies

Now that I've covered my background, why I love Amazon, shown you a couple real life example websites that I've been involved in, and shared how you can research niches, set up websites and write your content, I want to give you tips that you can apply while building your Amazon monetized niche and authority style websites. How you monetize your website with links from Amazon.com is one of the most important aspects of generating a solid income from your websites.

### Tip 1: Focus on links to products within the content

Well over 50% of my Amazon income came from simple text links inside the content of my website. So, what you'd want to do is go to the Amazon.com website and create text affiliate links with various calls to action for use inside the articles you've written on your website.

### The more links you can use in your content the better.

I generally do several links in the first paragraph of an article. For example:

*This product is $X.XX (link) and it's available in these four colors: Blue (link), Green (link), Yellow (link) and Pink (link).*

As you can see from just that example I've put in 5 affiliate links already but users won't be annoyed because I'm helping them by linking directly to different color options and showing them the price.

Here's another example:

*The product features a 46 inch screen, 1080p resolution, 240hz refresh rate and 3D capability (See Full Product Specs Here) (link)*

And another example and how I generally end my product oriented articles:

*Be Sure To Check out This Product on Amazon.com (link)*

Just remember, the more links you provide the more opportunities to get someone onto Amazon.com and once someone goes to Amazon through one of your affiliate links **you'll receive a commission on any product they purchase during the next 24 hours**. Now, the process for creating text affiliate links for your content can be a little tedious as you have to go to the Amazon.com website to get each of your text links; however, you can also use the EasyAzon Wordpress plugin to allow you to search for products on Amazon.com from inside your blog that you'd like to link to. I had this software built in mid 2011 and have been steadily improving it ever since – EasyAzon. I've got a $10 discount for Kindle book readers just as a thank you for buying my book which you can use here: http://easyazon.com/kindle-book-discount/ or you can use the free bonus I offered at the beginning of the book which is a lite version of EasyAzon: http://chrisguthriebooks.com/free-software/. Anytime I mention premium tools I want to reiterate that you don't need to buy anything extra besides domains and web hosting if you don't want to. I only make recommendations to help save you time and make things faster than doing it the free manual way.

### Tip 2: Make product images clickable

When using Wordpress you have the ability to upload images to use in your blog posts. The Wordpress default is that once you upload an image and select the size it will automatically include a link to that image (so that if you used a smaller size image website visitors can click the image to see a larger one, for instance). **Keeping the default is a huge wasted opportunity.** Instead, whenever you upload an image of a product use an Amazon affiliate link so that when people click that image they'll go to Amazon.com and give you another chance at earning a commission. In fact, you can even try to use the smaller image option as some visitors will click through because they want to see a larger version of the picture and when they do you'll have gotten them onto Amazon.com. I did an in depth study on some of my websites to see just how many people clicked images and then subsequently purchased something. It was over 10%! So, just this one tip alone could potentially add an extra 10% to your Amazon site earnings. *(If you opted to get the EasyAzon plugin at http://easyazon.com/kindle-book-discount/ you can easily upload images from within the plugin and have the affiliate link automatically added to the image.)*

### Tip 3: Use buy now call to action image buttons

In addition to linking to the product in the content and making the product images clickable I also like to include a "buy now" image button in my articles at the end of the content. To do this manually upload an Amazon buy image for use in your content near the end and then use an Amazon affiliate link for that buy now button image. If you need Amazon buy now call to action buttons I've created a page on my blog that you can go to so that you can download the buttons for use on your websites. The page includes buttons for every country that Amazon has an affiliate program in:

http://entrepreneurboost.com/amazon-order-buttons/

For years people have been conditioned by Amazon to click the buy button when they're on Amazon.com and they're interested in purchasing. So, if you use this button at the end of your content it's another method to help get them to purchase through one of your affiliate links. This is just one more way to get your web visitors to click through onto Amazon.com. *(Again, adding the buy now buttons is something EasyAzon can do for you as well if you don't want to do it manually).*

### Tip 4: Product review articles convert the best

Doing a quality product review for a product directly related to your niche is a very easy way to garner higher click-through rates and increased sales, but only if your review is high quality.

In an ideal scenario you contact the manufacturer's marketing team or PR agency using the tips I shared with you earlier in the previous section of this book to get a demo unit of the product to review. Unfortunately, this takes a lot of effort and may not be worth it on a smaller traffic site, at least at first.

During the review I like to go in depth on some of the various features and (more importantly) discuss how the product can satisfy various pains the customer might be having because they don't own the product yet. It really does help conversions if you try to pre-sell the visitors before they click through to Amazon.com via one of your affiliate links. Additionally, visitors are frequently looking at multiple different products and trying to decide which one is worth buying of the two or more choices. What I strongly recommend is to not only write reviews for the top products within your niche but also compare those top products to each other within your reviews. You can determine the top products in your niche by going to the Amazon.com website, searching for a product keyword like "video cards" then selecting the department (in this case electronics) and then selecting "Most Popular" from the drop down menu. The products that come up will give you a good list to start from.

However you decide to write your review the point is that you want to convince the reader to investigate their purchase options by the time they finish reading an article, which is why I always include links to all of the products mentioned in a review at the end of the article as well. That way it's an easy transition from learning about the product during your review and then at the end making a purchase.

### Tip 5: Push Amazon.com heavily during holiday shopping periods

During holiday time period's web visitors are less likely to be turned off by excessive product promotion because they know the best deals are available during these time periods. This tip is more applicable to authority style websites where content is likely to be created more frequently, but the point is that during the holidays you can get away being more aggressive with promoting products. The reason for this is because they'll view the product promotion as a service especially if the discount is severe and truly one time (which frequently happens during the lightning deals time frame found during Black Friday, Cyber Monday and Cyber Week). So be sure to constantly push products so that your visitors will see the best deals from you first and then you can get them onto Amazon.com so that anything they buy during the holidays for the next 24 hours you'll get a commission on.

My record earning days all came during the holidays when I'd typically make between $500 and $1,000 a day every day during Black Friday Week, Cyber Monday and Cyber Week. It is lower during other holidays like Mother's Day, Father's Day, Presidents Day, Valentine's Day etc. but you can still promote various sales during these holidays as well. I target every holiday because Amazon creates an actual dedicated sales page every time one of these holidays come around. The deals shared on these pages are generally really good too.

What I recommend doing is putting together an article of all the top products that are on sale in your niche using the tips I've shared earlier like linking as many times as possible and making the product image clickable. Then send out an email to your email list to get even more conversions (see tip 11).

**Tip 6: Sell more total quantity of products to make incrementally more money:**

This one sounds simple enough and it really is. The more you sell with Amazon's affiliate program the more you make AND the higher percentage you can earn. During holiday months I have hit around the 8% mark which is double the 4% rate you start with for shipping only 1 − 6 items per month. Even if you sold 7 items you get bumped up to 6% and the best part is that this increase in commission percentage is retroactive (meaning once you reach the next level you get to apply the higher percentage referral fee to every product you've sold during the entire month).

*This graph may have changed from the time you've read this book and I'll try to ensure it's always updated but this is found under the "Help" section of your Amazon Associates account.*

**Tip 7: Sell large quantities of inexpensive products to boost your payout on high priced products**

This tip is somewhat related to the previous one, but the idea is to help boost your commission rate up into the higher performance payouts. I have websites that are set up in lower competition niches where the items typically aren't as expensive and where it's easier to sell these products in larger quantities ($50 or less). I also have other websites that sell more expensive products such as 3D TV's ($XXX - $X,XXX) that are sold less frequently. This way I get to use the increased quantity of sales from these lower priced product websites to help me get up into higher payout brackets so instead of making 6% on that high end item I'll get closer to the 8.5% range instead.

*Note: Certain product categories only pay 4% regardless of quantity sold. You can see these categories in the Amazon Associates help section.*

**Tip 8: Create a product comparison grid of the top products**

Creating a product comparison grid for all of the products within your niche and allowing people to sort by various features is a great way to get some additional sales. I've used this tactic on several of my websites and the product comparison page alone can add an additional 5-10% income increase for a website or more. In fact, I'll repost the income stats from my 3D TV website and you can see that well over $2,000 in earnings came from the product comparison grid found here: http://3dtvreviews.org/3d-tv-comparison/

To create this product grid required a manual process (which admittedly is time consuming). I may create some software to do this in a more automated fashion in the future, but if you'd like to create a product comparison grid like the one I did you can do so with a free Wordpress plugin called "WP TablePress" (simply go to your Wordpress dashboard > plugins > search for plugins > type in "WP TablePress" hit search and then install). What I do is include various columns for information about the niche that is relevant. In this case it's the size of the TV, the display type (LCD vs LED etc.), refresh rate and of course price.

**SEO Bonus:** In this case "3D TV Comparison" is my target keyword phrase and in fact this is a frequently searched keyword phrase for most niches as well i.e. "Your Niche Comparison" so if you create a comparison you may be able to capture some additional search engine traffic for that keyword. Now it's important to mention that you're more likely to benefit from this SEO bonus if it's an authority site that you're building rather than a niche site. Remember – niche sites are more suited ranking for the one keyword phrase that you're targeting as opposed to many.

### Tip 9: Publish a daily or weekly deals post

If you want to find a way to be able to mention products that are on sale more frequently on your website, one of the easiest ways I've done that in the past is to just do a weekly deals post. What I'll do is publish a post every week with the best deals for my niche and then incorporate all of the previous tactics I've discussed above to link to those products on Amazon.com. Depending on how often you publish articles and your decision on a niche website or authority website strategy you could do it more or less frequently (I've seen some websites do these style of articles every day). You could always do a combination of both niche and authority style websites as well if you wanted to (that's what I did).

### Tip 10: Publish a monthly bestseller list

Amazon has a bestseller page found simply at http://amazon.com/bestsellers and so one thing I've done on my websites is publish a monthly bestsellers list and simply mention the currently trending bestsellers in my target niche. Generally speaking the cream rises to the top so if you write an article talking about the bestselling products those are likely to be the best products your visitors are looking to buy anyway. It's all about helping to pre-sell your visitors so that when they finish reading your content and click through one of the affiliate links you've used on your website they can make a decision to buy.

Just go to http://amazon.com/bestsellers and look for your respective niche category. When I write these articles I typically shoot for using the top 5 or top 10 products in my articles.

### Tip 11: Build an email list on your website

You can make a lot of money with an email list and receptive prospects. With niche and authority Amazon websites the bulk of the income will generally come from the website content, but there is still a lot of value in building an email list. One strategy to improve your conversion rates is to give away something for free on your website in order to get someone to sign up for your newsletter. This strategy is used by many a blogger and internet marketer and it works very well in niche and authority style Amazon websites when you're giving away something like a PDF buyer's guide. In the guide you can compare the various top products in your niche and then link back to the full reviews on your website *(it's against Amazon Affiliate Terms Of Service to use affiliate links in PDF's)*. If a buyer's guide doesn't fit your niche you can also use free reports, general information guides, explanations about the technology used in the product or any other useful information that will encourage people to sign up for your newsletter and email list.

Once you have people on your email list you want to use a follow-up sequence of emails and what I typically do is send them to my "money" pages, my best performers. In the case of the 3D TV website, a page that would fit would be the bestselling TV's of the month, or the 3D TV comparison grid. The purpose is to follow-up with them to see if they've made a purchase decision yet and to encourage them to make a decision to buy after reading some of your content and following through one of the links.

During the holidays I've done very well simply sending emails to my lists about the various Black Friday, Cyber Monday, Mother's Day etc.

deals that Amazon has going on. The newsletter service that I use and recommend is Aweber. It's under $20 a month to start but the price goes up as you add more subscribers. If you want to learn more about email marketing and building an email list you can check out this page on my blog:

http://entrepreneurboost.com/build-a-list/

### Tip 12: Look at other sites doing well with Amazon.com

Flippa.com is a marketplace where people buy and sell websites, and one thing you can do is look at websites that are making money with Amazon (which is generally disclosed on the income summary area) and then you can look at that website to see how they're monetizing it with Amazon. Again, this is something that the website owner will probably explain in the website listing and if they are operating in a similar niche as you, simply apply the tactics they're using to your own website. This may also help you come up with other ideas for websites that you can build. *If you want to read case studies on websites I've purchased then read my other book:http://chrisguthriebooks.com/book2*

### Tip 13: Use different tracking IDs for each website you own

Amazon allows you to create up to 100 tracking IDs in your affiliate account (and you can always ask for more if you need them). You should use a different ID for each of your websites so that you can track the income from each one and determine which websites are generating the most sales for you. This is a basic tip but I've seen people use the same tracking ID before so I wanted to make sure you knew to create at least one tracking ID for each website you create.

### Tip 14: Simply get visitors onto Amazon.com

No matter how you do it just try and get visitors onto Amazon.com and then let them do what they do best. Convert visitors into buyers. They've spent millions of dollars optimizing their homepage, product pages and checkout system all in an attempt to get people to go through with a transaction. Remember too that once you send someone to Amazon.com you get 24 hours to earn a commission on anything they buy. I've done some in depth analysis on my order reports and **I estimate 30% of my earnings came from products that aren't even related to**

**what I am selling on my websites**. This is just one of the extra benefits of simply getting visitors onto Amazon.com.

### Tip 15: Sign up for an Amazon account and get started

To sign up for an Amazon Associates account and join their affiliate program you need to have a functional website. Once you've followed the advice I shared in this blog and created your first website you can then apply to their affiliate program and add affiliate links to your content according to the tips I outlined.  Sign up for Amazon Associates here:

http://affiliate-program.amazon.com/

# 9. How to Get Started Today:

When I first started trying to make money online I tried a lot of different things and literally **wasted years spinning my wheels** with websites that would have never been successful. It wasn't until 2009 that my mindset shifted and I was able to finally break through and earn a respectable income online. If you'd like to learn more about my story you can listen to my first podcast episode where I explain in more detail how I started from scratch and built a six-figure business:http://entrepreneurboost.com/podcast-1-show-introduction-and-how-i-built-a-six-figure-online-business/. I hope that after reading this book you feel you've been given some actionable advice based on my real life experiences that you can apply towards building your own successful websites.

**One final reminder about my bonus offer:**

As I've illustrated in this book the one thing you absolutely must have is web hosting if you want to make money with websites. Because web hosting is the one thing that everyone needs, I want to give you a coupon to save money when you sign up for HostGator hosting. I will get a commission if you sign up using my coupon, but as a thank you from me I'll also give you free access to my powerful Azon Wordpress Theme which is a Wordpress theme that I use on http://wirelesshdmi.net,http://3dtvreviews.org and a bunch of other websites. I'll also give you access to some additional Amazon video training. If you want to take advantage of this offer simply follow these steps below.

Step 1: Go to http://entrepreneurboost.com/hostgator and when ordering your hosting use the coupon code "**kindlechris**" (no quotes) when you place your order to claim your savings

Step 2: Send an email to support@nicheprofitcourse.com along with the domain you used at sign up and I'll get you hooked up with the Azon Theme and the bonus training.

I have been a HostGator user for several years and I'm very pleased with them. Even if you don't take advantage of my offer they're a great hosting company to use for your niche or authority style websites.

Also don't forget to download my free software bonus. I spent several thousand dollars on the creation of this Amazon Wordpress plugin that you can use on every single one of your websites that you own (free unlimited site license): http://chrisguthriebooks.com/free-software/

Thank you again for reading through my book and if you have any comments or questions I'm personally available and would be happy to help you out. You can reach me via the link below:

http://entrepreneurboost.com/contact

To your success,

Chris Guthrie

EntrepreneurBoost.com

# 10. More Books By Chris Guthrie

*How To Invest In Online Real Estate*

In this book I show you the tactics and strategies necessary to buy websites and turn a profit as quickly as possible. As an investment strategy buying websites can provide an excellent ROI, but there are a lot of mistakes that beginners make that you can learn avoid by reading this book.

http://chrisguthriebooks.com/book2

*5 Proven Methods to Make $1,000+ Per Month With Websites*

This book is dedicated to giving you not only ideas, but tactics to build up websites that generate over $1,000 per month. Although Chris has experience with all 5 methods, he interviewed experts in each field to make sure you are getting the best information possible.

http://chrisguthriebooks.com/book3

Printed in Great Britain
by Amazon

36035548R00030